TABLE OF CONTENTS 4

MEET THE HUMPBACK WHALE

Humpback whales are among the largest animals on Earth. They live in the sea and sing songs that travel through the water. They have powerful bodies and sometimes leap above the water's surface. The humpback whale's name comes from a shape the animal makes with its back while diving.

Many kinds of animals fill the world. Mammals, birds, reptiles, insects, and fish are all types of animals. Because humpback whales live in the ocean, some people mistake them for fish. But whales are not fish. They are mammals.

Humpback whales are named for the way they arch their backs when diving.

All mammals share certain traits. Mammals are vertebrates, which means they have backbones. They are warm-blooded and have hair on their bodies. They also make milk for their babies. Yet each animal in the mammal group also has traits that make it unique. So humpback whales are not exactly like any other mammal in the world.

CHAPTER 1

WHAT DO HUMPBACK WHALES LOOK LIKE?

Humpback whales are large-bodied mammals. From the end of the snout to the tip of the tail, this whale reaches the length of a school bus. A humpback whale's body is also sleek and built for swimming. A powerful tail propels the whale forward. Flippers the size of minivans help with balance and steering.

Stringy material called baleen hangs from the roof of the humpback whale's mouth. To eat, the humpback whale opens its mouth wide and scoops in water. Grooves on the whale's throat expand to hold all the water. Then the whale pushes the water out through its lips. The baleen traps fish, plankton, and krill inside.

DID YOU KNOW?

The body of a humpback whale can reach **62 FEET** (19 meters) in length. The flippers can be as long as 16 feet (5 m).

The heads of these massive mammals have golf-ball-sized bumps and two blowholes on top. Before each dive, the humpback whale takes a deep breath through its blowholes. The whale can stay underwater for up to thirty minutes. When it returns to the surface, it breathes out through the blowholes. Onlookers can see the spray from miles away.

HUMPBACK WHALES VS. HUMPBACK DOLPHINS

Humpback dolphins also swim and dive in the ocean. Like humpback whales, humpback dolphins have tails and flippers for moving through water. Humpback dolphins also have streamlined bodies like humpback whales. But the bodies of humpback dolphins are smaller than the bodies of humpback whales. Some humpback dolphins have humps on their backs too.

A humpback dolphin uses a blowhole to take in oxygen. When the dolphin dives, it must hold its breath, as a humpback whale does. But a humpback dolphin has one blowhole on its head, not two. In between dives, the dolphin breathes in and out through this blowhole.

Like humpback whales, humpback dolphins eat fish and other ocean animals. But the mouths of humpback dolphins are different from the mouths of humpback whales. Humpback whales have baleen. Humpback dolphins have teeth. They chew their food before eating it.

This humpback dolphin has a smooth body and a hump on its back.

COMPARE IT!

HUMPBACK WHALES

VS.

HUMPBACK DOLPHINS

HUMPBACK WHALES		HUMPBACK DOLPHINS
52 TO 62 FEET (16 TO 19 M)	◄ MAXIMUM LENGTH ►	**9 FEET** (2.8 M)
80,000 POUNDS (36,290 KILOGRAMS)	◄ MAXIMUM WEIGHT ►	**570 POUNDS** (260 KG)

◄ TEETH ►

Stringy baleen for trapping fish

Pointy teeth for chewing

HUMPBACK WHALES VS. HEDGEHOGS

Hedgehogs are prickly mammals with pointed noses, short legs, and curved claws. You can find them in flower beds, vegetable gardens, and hedges. Hedgehogs are much smaller than humpback whales. A humpback can be as big as a school bus. A hedgehog can fit in a person's hand.

A hedgehog has a soft belly, but spiky hairs cover its back.

Both humpback whales and hedgehogs have hair. But a humpback whale has only a few hairs. A single hair grows from each golf-ball-sized bump on its head. The hairs may help the whale sense movement in the water and locate nearby prey.

A hedgehog has hair all over its body. Soft fur covers its belly. Thousands of spikes called quills cover its back. Believe it or not, the quills are a kind of hair. When threatened, the hedgehog tucks itself into a prickly ball. The sharp quills keep it safe from predators.

DID YOU KNOW?
Each of the hedgehog's **QUILLS** is filled with pockets of air separated by crisscrossing plates. This combination makes the quills lightweight but strong.

CHAPTER 2

WHERE HUMPBACK WHALES LIVE

Humpback whales swim throughout the oceans of the world.
They live near coastlines and islands. During summer, humpbacks
live in chilly waters near the North and South Poles. In these
waters, humpbacks fill up on plankton, shrimplike krill, and small
fish. Humpbacks store much of this food within their blubber (fat).

In fall, humpback whales leave their feeding grounds. They travel
great distances to reach warm waters near the equator. Once
humpback whales reach these waters, they mate and give birth.
And they live off the food they ate throughout the summer. In
spring, they return to their feeding grounds.

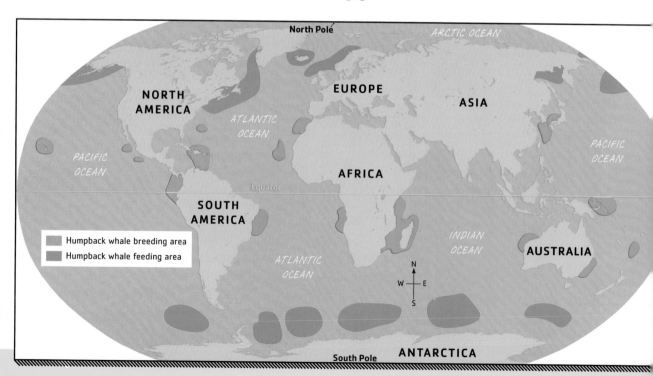

Humpback whales live in both warm and cold climates.

In the past, sailors killed large numbers of humpback whales. Whale meat and blubber were highly valuable. Humpbacks were in danger of disappearing forever. More recently, international laws have protected humpback whales. Many humpbacks once again inhabit the oceans.

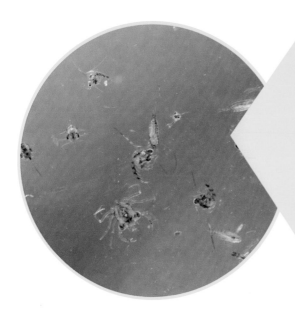

DID YOU KNOW?
A humpback whale can eat up to 2,000 pounds (900 kg) of **FOOD** a day in its feeding grounds.

HUMPBACK WHALES VS. GRAY WHALES

Whales swim in all the oceans of the world and in some rivers and lakes. They belong to a group of mammals that includes whales, dolphins, and porpoises. Whales come in different shapes and sizes. They all have streamlined bodies for swimming.

Gray whales live near coastlines in the Pacific Ocean. Like humpbacks, gray whales use their baleen to filter food. Unlike humpbacks, gray whales feed on the ocean floor. They roll on their sides, swim slowly, scoop mud in their mouths, and strain the mud for food.

Gray whales search for food at the bottom of the Pacific Ocean.

COMPARE IT!

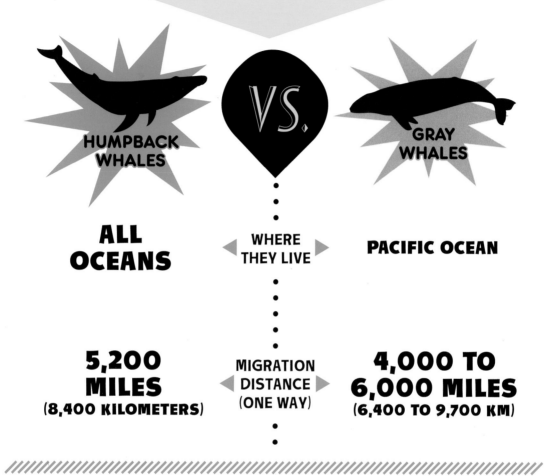

HUMPBACK WHALES	VS.	GRAY WHALES
ALL OCEANS	WHERE THEY LIVE	**PACIFIC OCEAN**
5,200 MILES (8,400 KILOMETERS)	MIGRATION DISTANCE (ONE WAY)	**4,000 TO 6,000 MILES** (6,400 TO 9,700 KM)

Like humpback whales, gray whales migrate long distances. In summer, they feed in cold waters off the coast of Alaska. In winter, they migrate to warmer waters, near Mexico. Gray whales mate and give birth while in these warm waters.

People once hunted gray whales. These whales are easy to catch because they swim slowly and close to shore. The widespread killing left few gray whales alive. Modern laws protect gray whales, and their population has grown.

HUMPBACK WHALES VS. FENNEC FOXES

Humpback whales live their entire lives in water, but fennec foxes are adapted for a habitat where water is scarce. The fennec fox is at home in one of the driest places in the world, the Sahara of Africa. The fox can go for a long time without drinking. It usually gets enough water from its food.

The desert landscape of the Sahara is hot during the day. A fennec fox's big ears give off heat and help keep the fox cool. They also help the fox hear its prey scratching in the desert sand. Humpback whales also can hear in their habitat. But their ears are tiny holes on the sides of their heads.

DID YOU KNOW?
The fennec fox has **FUR** on the bottom of its feet to help it walk on the Sahara's hot sand.

Although days in the Sahara are hot, the nights are cold. The fennec fox's thick fur shields the animal from the sun during the day and keeps it warm during the cold nights. This is very different from the way humpback whales stay warm. Humpbacks rely on a layer of blubber under their skin.

The fennec fox's thick fur protects it from the harsh desert sun.

CHAPTER 3

HUMPBACK WHALES IN ACTION

Humpback whales make noises that travel through the water. They use their mouths to moan and chirp. Scientists call these sounds songs. Only male humpbacks sing. All the males in one place sing the same song. No one knows why male humpbacks sing. Maybe singing is a way to attract females. Maybe singing is a way to challenge other males.

Humpback whales travel in groups called pods.

Humpback whales interact in other ways too. They use their bodies for acrobatics. They leap from the water and come down with giant splashes. They slap their fins. They smack their tails on the water. The whales may use their acrobatics for communication, courtship, or play.

At their feeding grounds, humpback whales work together to catch fish. The whales circle around a school of fish. They blow bubbles at the same time, making a net that traps fish in one spot. Then the whales lunge and swallow huge mouthfuls of their prey.

HUMPBACK WHALES VS. GIBBONS

Gibbons are the smallest of the apes. These mammals live in the **rain forests** of Asia. They have long arms and slender, furry bodies. Although gibbons live in the jungle, not in the ocean, they share some surprising traits with humpback whales.

Humpbacks are acrobats of the ocean. They leap from the water into the air. They slap their tails and fins against the water's surface. Gibbons are acrobats of the trees. They use their long arms to swing between branches. They jump from branch to branch or from tree to tree.

Gibbons have long arms to help them swing between tree branches.

Both humpback whales and gibbons are known as musical mammals. Male and female gibbons make loud calls. The sounds are called songs. A male-and-female pair starts the morning by whooping and howling. The gibbons continue singing as they move through their **territory**. Singing is a way to send other gibbons a message. The sounds warn other gibbons to stay away.

COMPARE IT!

HUMPBACK WHALES

GIBBONS

OCEANS OF THE WORLD

◄ WHERE THEY LIVE ►

RAIN FORESTS OF ASIA

◄ WHO SINGS ►

ONLY MALES

MALES AND FEMALES

PROBABLY TO COURT FEMALES AND COMPETE WITH MALES

◄ WHY THEY SING ►

TO MARK THEIR HOME TERRITORY

HUMPBACK WHALES VS. SLOTHS

Sloths live in rain forests in Central and South America. These mammals spend their lives in the trees. Not only do sloths and humpback whales have different habitats, they also have very different behaviors. Sloths don't move around much. Instead, they hang upside down from tree branches for hours at a time.

Sloths spend much of their time hanging from trees.

Sloths like to remain still as they eat leaves. They move so slowly that algae grow on their shaggy fur, giving the fur a greenish color. This behavior helps protect sloths from predators. Slowness makes these mammals hard to spot. The greenish algae on their fur help them blend in with the trees.

Sloths also don't travel far. Unlike humpback whales, which can swim distances of many miles, sloths rarely come down from the trees. On land, they can only crawl. They dig their front claws into the ground and drag their bodies forward.

Sloths and humpback whales do have one surprising trait in common. Both are good swimmers. Sloths sometimes fall out of trees into rivers. Their strong front arms help them swim to shore.

Both humpback whales and sloths are good swimmers. Sloths use their strong front arms to move through water.

CHAPTER 4

THE LIFE CYCLE OF HUMPBACK WHALES

Humpback whales can live for fifty years or longer. They begin life in warm tropical waters. A humpback whale calf is born tail first. Its mother helps it swim to the surface to take its first breath.

The calf and its mother develop a strong bond. They swim together and often touch each other with their flippers. The calf nurses on its mother's rich milk. This milk helps the humpback calf grow rapidly. When the calf is one year old, it is ready to eat fish and krill.

DID YOU KNOW?

At birth, a humpback **CALF** is 10 to 15 feet (3 to 4.5 m) long and weighs a ton (0.9 metric tons).

A whale calf is able to swim at birth.

At ten years old, a humpback whale has finished growing. It carries many traits it has inherited from its parents. It has a huge body made for swimming and baleen for filtering prey. It can work with other humpbacks to catch fish in bubble nets. If it is a male, it can sing complex songs. All of these traits help humpback whales survive.

HUMPBACK WHALES VS. CARIBOU

Caribou are another kind of mammal. These wild reindeer live in the north all around the world. They migrate long distances each year. These mammals have a similar life cycle to humpback whales.

Caribou migrate long distances in search of food.

A day-old caribou calf nuzzles with its mother.

During summer, a female caribou gives birth, usually to one calf. Like baby humpbacks, newborn caribou can keep up with their mothers right away. A caribou calf can follow its mother within an hour of being born. In only a week, the calf can run fast enough to keep away from predators.

A strong bond between mother and calf helps young humpbacks stay safe from predators. The same is true of caribou. The caribou mother calls to her calf, and the calf learns her sound. Caribou calves nurse from their mothers for about a year, about the same length as humpback whales. But caribou reach adulthood at the age of two, sooner than humpbacks. Caribou live as long as fifteen years.

HUMPBACK WHALES VS. HOUSE MICE

The house mouse is a small mammal. It can fit in a teacup. The house mouse lives wherever people live. It inhabits buildings such as houses, barns, and stores. The house mouse does not just differ from the humpback whale in size and habitat. It has a different life cycle too.

Unlike humpback whales, house mice are born in litters. Each litter contains between three and twelve babies. A female mouse can have as many as ten litters in one year. That's a lot of baby mice!

Unlike baby humpbacks, newborn mice come into the world helpless. They are naked, and their eyes are closed. Two weeks will pass before they are ready to open their eyes. But baby mice grow up more quickly than humpback whales. Three weeks after birth, house mice are ready to stop nursing and are able to eat solid food. Humpback babies nurse for a full year. When house mice are two months old, they are already fully grown. But humpback whales don't reach adult size until they are ten years old.

Young house mice are fully grown at two months old.

COMPARE IT!

HUMPBACK WHALES

VS.

HOUSE MICE

1 CALF	AVERAGE NUMBER OF YOUNG AT BIRTH	5 TO 6 PUPS
1 CALF BORN EVERY 2 TO 3 YEARS	BIRTH RATE	5 TO 10 LITTERS PER YEAR
77 YEARS	TYPICAL LIFE SPAN	2 YEARS

HUMPBACK WHALE TRAIT CHART

This book explored the way the humpback whale is similar to and different from some other mammals. What other mammals would you add to the list?

	WARM-BLOODED	HAIR ON BODY	GIVES BIRTH TO LIVE YOUNG	FLIPPERS	MIGRATES LONG DISTANCES	ABLE TO MOVE ABOUT AT BIRTH
HUMPBACK WHALE	X	X	X	X	X	X
HUMPBACK DOLPHIN	X	X	X	X		X
HEDGEHOG	X	X	X			
GRAY WHALE	X	X	X	X	X	X
FENNEC FOX	X	X	X			
GIBBON	X	X	X			
SLOTH	X	X	X			
CARIBOU	X	X	X		X	X
HOUSE MOUSE	X	X	X			

GLOSSARY

acrobatics: stunts involving difficult movements such as flips

adapted: suited to living in a particular environment

blubber: a thick layer of fat under the skin of whales and other sea mammals. Blubber provides warmth and stores energy.

communication: the sharing of information

equator: an imaginary circle around Earth equally distant from the North Pole and the South Pole

habitat: an environment where an animal naturally lives. A habitat is the place where an animal can find food, water, air, shelter, and a place to raise its young.

krill: small, shrimplike plankton that live in the sea. Krill are a major source of food for baleen whales.

plankton: tiny animals and plants that float in bodies of water

population: all the members of one type of animal living in a particular place

predators: animals that hunt other animals

prey: animals that are hunted by a predator for food

rain forests: forests of tall trees that receive high amounts of rain. Rain forests are usually found in tropical areas.

territory: an area that is occupied and defended by an animal or a group of animals

traits: features that an animal inherits from its parents. Body size and fur color are examples of traits.

warm-blooded: able to maintain a constant body temperature that is usually warmer than the surrounding environment

LERNER

Expand learning beyond the printed book. Download free, complementary educational resources for this book from our website, www.lerneresource.com.

SOURCE

SELECTED BIBLIOGRAPHY

"Animal Diversity Web." University of Michigan Museum of Zoology. April 27, 2014. http://animaldiversity.ummz.umich.edu/.

"Cetaceans: Whales, Dolphins, and Porpoises." NOAA Fisheries Office of Protected Resources. April 24, 2014. http://www.nmfs.noaa.gov/pr/species/mammals/cetaceans/.

Elphick, Jonathan, Steve Parker, David Burnie, and Christopher Norris. *Mammal.* New York: Dorling Kindersley, 2003.

"Fact Sheets." American Cetacean Society. April 24, 2014. http://acsonline.org/fact-sheets/.

Macdonald, David. *The Encyclopedia of Mammals.* New York: Facts on File, 2001.

Reilly, S. B, J. L. Bannister, J. L. Best, P. B. Brown, M. Brownell Jr., R. L. Butterworth, D. S. Chapham et al. *"Megaptera novaeangliae."* IUCN. April 23, 2014. http://www.iucnredlist.org.

"Wildscreen Arkive." Wildscreen. April 22, 2014. http://www.arkive.org/details/13006/0.

FURTHER INFORMATION

Fleischer, Paul. *Ocean Food Webs in Action.* Minneapolis: Lerner Publications, 2014. Pick up this book to discover what different ocean animals eat and how each animal's eating habits affect other animals.

Humpback Whales: Frequently Asked Questions
http://www.learner.org/jnorth/search/HumpbackWhale.html
Do you have questions about humpback whales? Check out this site for more information about these musical mammals.

National Geographic—Humpback Meal
http://video.nationalgeographic.com/video/whale_humpback
Watch this video to hear humpback whales sing and to see them catching krill and plankton.

NOAA Fisheries—Whales: The Kids' Times
http://www.nmfs.noaa.gov/pr/education/whales.htm
Want to learn more about humpbacks, gray whales, and other whales? Take a trip to this site.

Webb, Sophie. *Far from Shore: A Naturalist Explores the Deep Ocean.* Boston: Houghton Mifflin Books for Children, 2011. Learn more about ocean animals as a scientist counts, collects, and observes underwater life.

INDEX